Bob Chilcott

Anthems 1

10 anthems for mixed voices

T0056047

MUSIC DEPARTMENT

OXFORD
UNIVERSITY PRESS

OXFORD

UNIVERSITY PRESS

Great Clarendon Street, Oxford OX2 6DP, England
198 Madison Avenue, New York, NY10016, USA

Oxford University Press is a department of the University of Oxford.
It furthers the University's aim of excellence in research, scholarship,
and education by publishing worldwide

20

ISBN 978-0-19-353089-8

Music origination by Barnes Music Engraving Ltd., East Sussex
Printed in Great Britain on acid-free paper by
Caligraving Ltd., Thetford, Norfolk.

Contents

For Julian Elloway, on his retirement from
Oxford University Press, December 2000

And Thank Him Then

Early 16th century

BOB CHILCOTT

Printed in Great Britain

OXFORD UNIVERSITY PRESS, MUSIC DEPARTMENT, GREAT CLARENDON STREET, OXFORD OX2 6DP

poco rit.

11 *mf*

God's pro-vi-dence for sus-te-nance it is for man;—

15 **a tempo** *mp*

Then we al-ways— to him give praise, and thank_ him then,—

18

— and thank_ him then.—

22

S.
A.

mp

Plea-sure it is— to hear, i - wis, the

T.
B.

mp

birds___ sing;___ The deer in the dale,__ the sheep in the vale, the corn___ spring - ing.___

God's pro - vi - dence for sus - te - nance it is for man;___

God's pro - vi - dence for sus - te - nance it is for man;___

Then we al - ways_ to him give praise, and thank_ him then,_____

_ and thank_ him then,_____ and

thank_ him then.

To the memory of William Chambers

Be thou my vision

Early Irish
tr. Mary Byrne (1880–1931)
versified Eleanor Hull (altered) (1860–1935)

BOB CHILCOTT

A version of this piece (BC43) with piano accompaniment is available separately (ISBN 0–19–343292–7).
An orchestral accompaniment is available for hire, scored for Fl., Ob., 2 Cl. in B♭, 2 Hn. in F, Harp, and Strings.

I thy true son;___ Be thou in me dwell-ing, and

Fa - ther, I__ thy_ son; Be with me, and

I with thee one._____

poco rit. **Tempo I**

SOPRANO SOLO *p espress.*

Be_ thou and thou on - ly the_

Even such is time

Sir Walter Ralegh (?1554–1618)

BOB CHILCOTT

Also available separately: BC11; ISBN 0-19-343208-0
This piece may be sung as a companion to *Love* BC10.

16

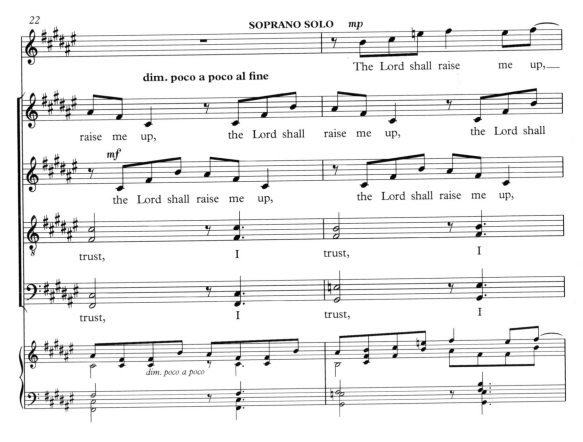

Commissioned in memory of Dan and Pat Jacobson by Jeanne Jacobson Stephens and Gary Stephens for the Lovers Lane United Methodist Sanctuary Choir, Dallas, Texas

God so loved the world

John 3: 16

BOB CHILCOTT

Also available separately: BC29; ISBN 0-19-343276-5

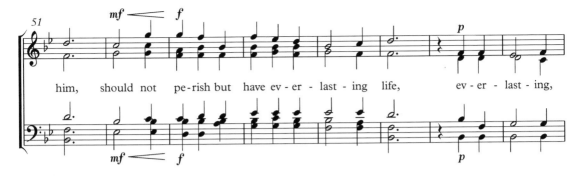

him, should not pe-rish but have ev-er-last-ing life, ev-er-last-ing,

SOLO SOPRANO *p*

ev - er - last - ing life, ev - er -

ev - er - last - ing, God so loved the world,____

ev - er - last - ing life.____ God so

-last - ing life, God so loved the world.

___ God so loved the world, so loved the world.

loved the world,____ God so loved the world.

For Mark Toews and the Lawrence Park Community Church Choir, Toronto

If ye love me

John 14: 15–17

BOB CHILCOTT

28

For Grupo Vocal Olisipo

Irish Blessing

Traditional

BOB CHILCOTT

Also available separately: BC18; ISBN 0-19-343229-3

And un-til we meet a - gain, _____

May God hold you, may God hold you, e - ver in the

palm of his hand. _____

SOPRANO
ALTO
May the road rise to meet you, _____ may the wind be e-ver at your
TENOR
BASS

back, may the sun shine warm u-pon your face, and the

rain fall soft u-pon your fields, _____ And un-til we meet a-

T. your fields,

cresc.

gain, _____ may God hold you,

dolce **S.** hold you, (div.) may God

April 1997

Just as I am

Charlotte Elliot (1789–1871)

BOB CHILCOTT

Also available separately: BC6; ISBN 0-19-351149-5

O Lamb __ of God, I come. ____

SOPRANO Just as I am, thou wilt re- ceive, wilt

ALTO Just as __ I am, thou __ wilt re- ceive, __

wel-come, par - don, cleanse, re - lieve, be - cause thy pro - mise

wilt wel-come, par - don, __ cleanse, __ re - lieve, be - cause __ thy pro - mise

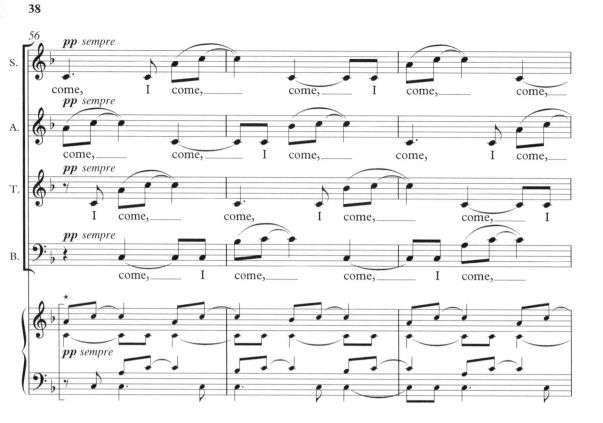

* Keyboard reduction for rehearsal only.

Song

Gerard Manley Hopkins (1844–89)

BOB CHILCOTT

* The horn part can be found on pages 50 and 51, and may be enlarged on a photocopier if required.

A slightly different arrangement of this piece can be found as the second movement of *Jubilate* by Bob Chilcott, BC26; ISBN 0-19-355827-0.

11

p
What I know of thee I bless,___ As ac-know-ledg-ing thy stress On my

mp espress.

p *cresc.*

14

be - ing and as see - ing Some-thing of thy ho - li - ness.___

dim.

poco stringendo

16 *mp cresc.*

Once I turned from thee and hid, Bound on what thou hast for-bid;___

poco stringendo

mp cresc.

sow the wind___ I would; I sinned:___ I re -

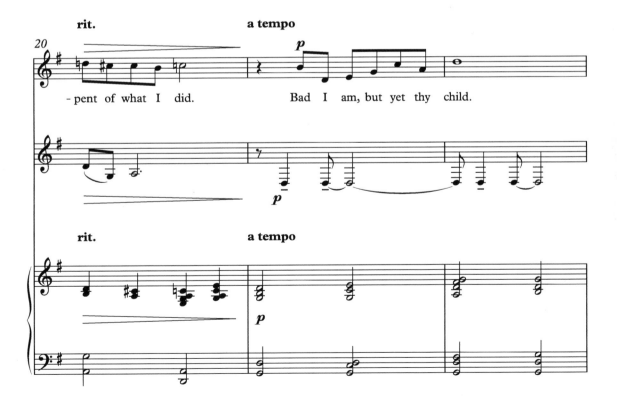

-pent of what I did. Bad I am, but yet thy child.

Fa-ther, be thou re-con-ciled. Spare thou me, since I see____ With thy might that thou art

poco stringendo

mild. I have life left with me still And thy pur-pose to ful-fill;—

poco stringendo

Yea a debt to pay thee yet: Help me, sir, and so I will.

But thou bidst and just thou art,_____ Me show mer-cy from my heart To-wards my

bro-ther, ev'-ry oth-er Man_ my mate and coun-ter-part,_ to-wards my

dim. e rit.　　　　　　　　**a tempo**

bro- ther_ ev'- ry oth - er Man　my　mate　and　count - er - part.

SOPRANO

ALTO

Thee, God,　I come from, to thee

TENOR

BASS

bro-ther, ev'-ry oth-er Man— my mate and coun-ter-part,— to-wards my

bro-ther,— ev'-ry oth-er Man my mate and coun - ter-part.

For Simon Carrington

Song

HORN PART

Gerard Manley Hopkins (1844–89)

BOB CHILCOTT

This and the following page may be enlarged on a photocopier if required.

*Commissioned in 2001 by The Vaulkhard Choral Trust
for the Choir Schools' Association*

Sweet Prospect

Samuel Stennett (1727–95)

BOB CHILCOTT

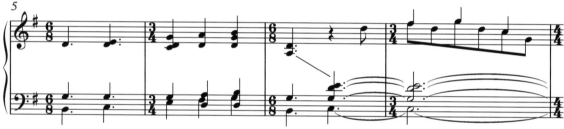

Also available separately: BC53; ISBN 0-19-343303-6

cast a wish - ful eye,_____ To__ Ca - naan's fair and

hap - py__ land, where my pos - sess - ions__ lie. O__

the trans - port - ing, rap - turous scene, that__ ri - ses to__ my

sight,_____ Sweet___ fields ar - rayed___ in li - ving___ green, and___

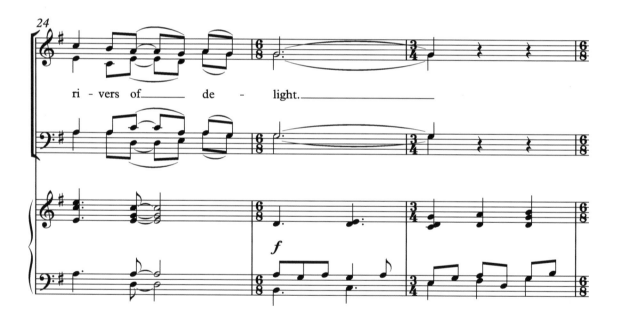

ri - vers of_____ de - light._____ and___

li - ving green, and ri -vers of_ de - light._

li - ving green, and_ ri -vers of_ de - light._

ff

Solo Reed

ff

No_

ff

chill - ing winds or pois - 'nous breath can reach that health - ful

(non solo)

shore; Sick - ness and sor - row, pain and death, are

felt and feared no more. O the trans - port - ing,

rap-turous scene, that_ ri - ses to_ my sight,_____ Sweet_

fields ar - rayed_ in li - ving_ green, and_ ri - vers of_____ de -

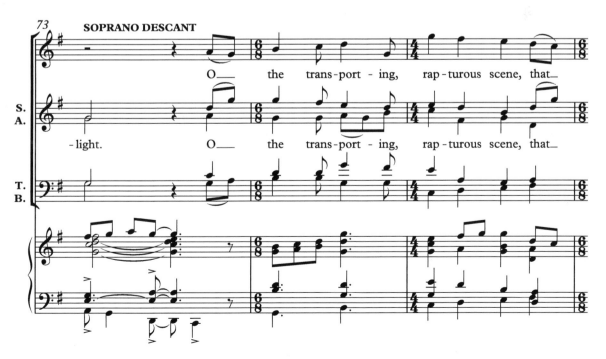

SOPRANO DESCANT

O___ the trans-port - ing, rap-turous scene, that_

-light. O___ the trans-port - ing, rap-turous scene, that_

S.
A.

T.
B.

For Terry Price and the Sanctuary Choir of Preston Hollow Presbyterian Church,
Dallas, Texas

Walk Softly

Early Shaker anthem

BOB CHILCOTT

down we will re - joice   And when we   hear   the Shep - herd's

gen - tle voice   We   will walk soft - ly,   soft - ly,____

soft - - ly,   We will walk   soft - - ly.